The limerick packs laughs anatomical
Into space that is quite economical.
  But the good ones I've seen
  So seldom are clean
And the clean ones so seldom are comical.

BANTAM BOOKS BY LARRY WILDE

THE LARRY WILDE BOOK OF LIMERICKS
THE OFFICIAL LAWYERS JOKE BOOK
THE OFFICIAL DOCTORS JOKE BOOK
More THE OFFICIAL SEX MANIACS JOKE BOOK
THE *Last* OFFICIAL JEWISH JOKE BOOK

also by the author

THE OFFICIAL POLISH JOKE BOOK
THE OFFICIAL ITALIAN JOKE BOOK
THE OFFICIAL JEWISH/IRISH JOKE BOOK
THE OFFICIAL VIRGINS/SEX MANIACS JOKE BOOK
THE OFFICIAL BLACK FOLKS/WHITE FOLKS JOKE BOOK
More THE OFFICIAL POLISH/ITALIAN JOKE BOOK
THE OFFICIAL DEMOCRAT/REPUBLICAN JOKE BOOK
THE OFFICIAL RELIGIOUS/*Not So* RELIGIOUS JOKE BOOK
THE OFFICIAL SMART KIDS/DUMB PARENTS JOKE BOOK
THE OFFICIAL GOLFERS JOKE BOOK
THE *Last* OFFICIAL POLISH JOKE BOOK
THE OFFICIAL DIRTY JOKE BOOK
THE OFFICIAL CAT LOVERS/DOG LOVERS JOKE BOOK
THE *Last* OFFICIAL ITALIAN JOKE BOOK
More THE OFFICIAL JEWISH/IRISH JOKE BOOK
THE OFFICIAL BOOK OF SICK JOKES
More THE OFFICIAL SMART KIDS/DUMB PARENTS JOKE
    BOOK
More THE OFFICIAL DEMOCRAT/REPUBLICAN JOKE BOOK
THE OFFICIAL BEDROOM/BATHROOM JOKE BOOK

and in hardcover

THE GREAT COMEDIANS TALK ABOUT COMEDY
HOW THE GREAT COMEDY WRITERS CREATE LAUGHTER
THE COMPLETE BOOK OF ETHNIC HUMOR

THE LARRY WILDE BOOK OF LIMERICKS

LARRY WILDE

Illustrations by Ron Wing

BANTAM BOOKS
TORONTO · NEW YORK · LONDON · SYDNEY

DEDICATED TO:

My friend
Sidney Miller, actor, writer,
producer, director, and the best
limerick lyricist since Lear.
(And I don't mean Norman.)

THE LARRY WILDE BOOK OF LIMERICKS
A Bantam Book / June 1982

Illustrations by Ron Wing

ISBN 0-553-20811-X

Published simultaneously in the United States and Canada

PRINTED IN THE UNITED STATES OF AMERICA

0 9 8 7 6 5 4 3 2 1

CONTENTS

Introduction

There are many techniques for extracting laughter. Slapstick, a practical joke, a funny face, a teasing remark, or the telling of a new gag are all used to delight and entertain friends, neighbors, and co-workers. But of all humor forms, perhaps the most popular is the limerick.

A limerick, basically, is a short joke or anecdote in rhyming verse element. This very factor may well be the main reason for its popularity down through the years. Many persons complain, "I can't seem to remember jokes," or, "I always forget the punch line." But when the joke is in meter, it requires the teller to learn and recite it exactly as written. Rhythm is the key to delivery, and delivery—as every professional comedian will attest—is essential to making people laugh.

How did this delightful, fanciful form of humor come about?

Humor historians disagree emphatically about the origin of the limerick. Some insist on a connection with the Irish town of Limerick. However, the consensus is that the five-line verse came from Ireland by way of France and then was popularized in England during the nineteenth century by Edward Lear.

Lear wrote 212 specimens, and although he called them "nonsense rhymes," Lear is considered the "father of the limerick." The following verse appeared in his *Book of Nonsense,* published in 1846:

There was a Young Lady of Norway
Who casually sat in a doorway;
When the door squeezed her flat
She exclaimed, "What of that?"
This courageous Young Lady of Norway.

By today's standards, this example of Lear's wit may not be a rib breaker, but the style set the pattern for many years to come. And then, around the turn of the century, a startling cultural development took place:

2

the fifth line of the limerick became risqué, even obscene. Over one hundred years later, we see the comedic evolution of Lear's original:

There was a young lady of Norway
Who hung by her heels in a doorway.
She said to her beau,
"Look at me, Joe,
I think I've discovered one more way."

Perhaps the most significant aspect of the limerick's long affair with lovers of wit is the *content*, a point aptly made in limerick form:

The limerick packs laughs anatomical
Into space that is quite economical.
But the good ones I've seen
So seldom are clean,
And the clean ones so seldom are comical.

A *Psychology Today* survey revealed to the general public what professional humorists have long known: the most desirable gag topic, without question, is sex. (Ethnicity came in second.) Even in an era of sexual awareness, erotica still titillates, and funny stories about lechery, lewdness, and lasciviousness get the biggest laughs:

The limerick's an art form complex
Whose contents run chiefly to sex.
   It's famous for virgins'
   And masculine urgin's
And swarms with erotic effects.

The question of taste then arises. What is acceptable, and what becomes unpleasant or disagreeable? Evidently, someone made a decision and gave birth to another limerick:

Said a printer well known for his wit:
"There are certain bad words we omit.
   It would sully our art
   To print the word f——,
And we never, oh, never, say sh——!"

As a matter of record, many limericks have passed the border of bawdiness into the realm of the obscene. Down through the years, there have been numerous collections of this sort published by various private clubs and academicians. The two most important modern-day author-enthusiasts are Clifford M. Crist and Gershon Legman.

Crist, a Ph.D. who taught at Princeton and later worked for academic publishers, is considered the consummate authority on limericks. A lifelong collector and a member of the famed Chicago *Society of the Fifth Line,* Crist performed an incalculable service as editor of the *Playboy Book of Limericks.*

Legman, an internationally recognized author, editor, and educator, collected, categorized, and commented on thousands of the classic five-line rhymes and published them in two separate volumes. For this monumental accomplishment, humor historians will be eternally grateful. (Legman will also be accorded sainthood in humor heaven for his two volumes *Rationale of the Dirty Joke* and *No Laughing Matter* in which he meticulously and intelligently analyzes erotic comedy material for its psychological and social content.)

Just as technology, medicine, law, engineering, et al. must grow in order to survive, so must humor. Something fresh has to arrive on the scene in order for it to endure. And, in fact, there is always something new in humor. Incredibly, after thirty years in the field of comedy, I still hear new jokes almost every day.

True, many of them are rewrites, switches, or different tacks on an old joke, but most are as fresh as new spring flowers. Such is the case with limericks. The following has been making the rounds since the small, expensive sports car Corvette first zoomed out of Detroit:

There once was a fellow named Brette
Loved a girl in his brand-new Corvette;
We know it's absurd,
But the last that we heard
They hadn't untangled them yet.

Now if you're putting together a book of limericks, it is essential to include specimens "fresh as spring flowers." One method is to do a switch on content or theme:

A high-flying pilot named Rhett
Screwed a stew in the Loo of a jet.
Though the plane has arrived
And the crews' clearly strived,
They haven't untangled them yet.

Coming up with one brand-new limerick based on a previous concept should, under normal circumstances, more than satisfy the author's ego. But sometimes another idea will jog the brain, insisting on a different notion. Here's another creation impelled by the classic Corvette:

A Grosse Point preppy named Bette
Loved a boy in her classic Corvette.
She said, "It's absurd,
Even though you're a nerd,
My panties are really quite wet!"

By the time you've finished this *Book of Limericks*, you will have surely thought of a number of ideas to put into rhyme. It will be great fun finding just the right word and an even greater delight to hear friends laughing at the result.

The next time you say, "Here's one I heard . . ." or "Listen to my version . . ." you will have become a contributor to the oral tradition that has made the limerick an intrinsic part of our humor folklore.

This verbal passing on of the five-liners unfortunately doesn't allow for the author's name to be included. Thus, a great majority of verses written by clever, witty people are lost in literary antiquity.

A recent collection of limericks by academic Ray Allen Billington is actually entitled *Limericks Historical and Hysterical, Plagiarized, Arranged, Annotated, and Some Written.*

Acknowledging and giving credit to the writers of all limericks is an impossible task. This book contains originals from many sources, including family and colleagues as well as classic examples that are old favorites.

I am particularly indebted to that ubiquitous contributor to literature: Anon.

However, if I have inadvertently omitted any author, I hereby offer sincere apologies.

Now, you say, you can't wait to get started on some giggles? You say you're anxious to find some old five-line friends you might have forgotten? You say you're dyin' to discover new rhymes so you can be the life of the party? Tell ya what I'm gonna do! I'm gonna shut up and let you get started laughing through limerick land.

LARRY WILDE
Los Angeles

Nonsense Nifties

There was a New Yorker named Billy
Who acted remarkably silly.
    At an All-Nations Ball,
    Dressed in nothing at all,
He claimed that his costume was Chile.

There was a young steno named Mallory
Who started to count every calorie.
  Said her boss in disgust,
  "If you lose half your bust,
Then you're worth only half of your salary."

* * *

An old spinster who died near Peekskill
Wrote a very queer clause in her will.
  It read: "To the priest,
  I leave my false teeth,
And now he can eat to his fill!"

* * *

There once was a newlywed bride
Who ate a green apple and died.
  The apple fermented
  Inside the lamented
And made cider inside her inside.

* * *

A Polack who lived near Champlain
Had his two legs cut off by a train.
   When they wept, "Oh, how sad!"
   He cried, "I be glad.
See, they've cut off my varicose vein!"

* * *

There was an old man named MacLeith
Who sat on his set of false teeth.
   He cried with a start,
   "Oh, Lord, bless my heart!
I've bitten myself underneath!"

* * *

An Italian named Sal Genovese
Was troubled a lot with black fleas,
   They filled up his bed
   And infested his head,
And don't ask me where else, if you please!

* * *

There was an old spinster named Wynn
Who was so uncommonly thin
　　That when she would drink,
　　As quick as a wink,
She'd slip through the straw and fall in.

* * *

A babe seeking beach souvenirs
Once suddenly burst into tears.
When they asked her the reason,
She said, "I have fleas on—
My ass and my boobs and my ears."

* * *

There was a kind man of Fort Worth
Who was born on the day of his birth.
He was married, some say,
On his wife's wedding day,
And he died when he quitted the earth.

* * *

A silly young man name of Clyde
In a funeral procession was spied.
When asked, "Who is dead?"
He giggled and said,
"I don't know, I just came for the ride."

* * *

"Oh, doctor," moaned rich Mrs. Monkshire,
"My crotch throbs. Please try acupuncture."
    Doc hauled out his pin
    And stuck it right in.
Things really got good at that juncture!

* * *

A Chicago steno named Alice
Had an ass as big as a palace.
    Her dresses were tight,
    And she made quite a sight,
To quicken the pulse of the callous.

* * *

A musician who played the bass fiddle
Once asked of a gal, "Do you diddle?"
    She replied, "Yes, I do
    But prefer it with two.
It's twice as much fun in the middle."

15

* * *

While dining, a man we'll call Hugh
Found a large mouse in the stew.
   Said the waiter, "Don't shout
   And wave it about,
Or the rest will be wanting one, too!"

16

* * *

An elderly former marine
Who grew so abnormally lean
   And flat and compressed
   That his back squeezed his chest,
And sideways he couldn't be seen.

* * *

The delighted, incredulous bride
Exclaimed to her groom at her side,
   "I never could quite
   Believe 'til tonight,
Our anatomies would coincide!"

* * *

A dear Dayton couple of taste
Were beautiful down to the waist,
   So they limited love
   To the regions above
And thus remained perfectly chaste.

* * *

There was a young man named Paul
Who fell in the spring in the fall;
  T'would have been a sad thing
  If he died in the spring,
But he didn't—he died in the fall.

* * *

An eccentric old fellow named Roffin
Once remarked in a bad fit of coughin',
  "It isn't the cough
  That carries you off.
It's the coffin they carry you off in."

* * *

There was an old watchman named Dill
Who took an atomical pill.
  His navel corroded;
  His backside exploded,
And they found his two nuts in Brazil.

* * *

There was a cute waitress named Hannah
Who slipped on a peel of banana.
    As she lay on her side,
    More stars she espied
Than there are in the Star Spangled Banner.

* * *

A pansy who used strong perfume
Once kept a baboon in his room.
   "It reminds me," he said,
   "Of a friend who is dead,"
But he never would tell us of whom.

* * *

There was a bank teller named Gail
Who turned most exceedingly pale.
   For a mouse climbed her leg,
   Don't repeat this, I beg . . .
And a splinter got caught in its tail.

* * *

There once lived a man in Slavonia
Whose mother-in-law had pneumonia.
   He hoped for the worst,
   And since April first,
She is sleeping beneath a begonia.

* * *

There was a stout fellow named Sydney
Who drank till he ruined his kidney.
  It shriveled and shrank
  As he sat there and drank
But he had a good time at it, didn't he?

* * *

There once was a man in his prime
Who lived with three wives at one time.
  When asked, "Why the third?"
  He replied, "One's absurd,
And bigamy, sir, is a crime!"

* * *

There was a young bachelor named Price
Who remarked, "Although bigamy's nice,
  Even two are a bore.
  I'd prefer three or four,
For the plural of spouse it is spice."

* * *

A Denver pro diver named Dree
Makes jumps which the crowd pays to see.
  Once he plunged from an oak,
  Drawing cheers from the folk,
For his shorts remained hung in the tree.

A plump Polish girl once said, "Why
Can't I look in my ear with my eye?
  If I put my mind in it,
  I'm sure I can do it.
You never can tell till you try."

A superstacked model named Jayne
Undressed by herself in a train.
  A saucy old porter
  Saw more than he oughter
And asked her to do it again!

* * *

He slyly unhooked her brassiere
As he nuzzled and nibbled her ear.
  He spread wide her thighs,
  Then to her surprise,
Hollered out, "April Fool—I'm a queer!"

* * *

A palmist whose readings were fiction
Was awed by her landlord's prediction:
  "I won't have a qualm
  If you don't cross my palm
With the rent, you'll face certain eviction."

* * *

Said Kay to her mother, "I fear
My husband's turned into a queer.
  On Sundays and Mondays
  He irons my undies,
And each evening he wears my brassiere."

* * *

There was an old couple from Mayville
Whose habits were quite medieval;
   They would strip to the skin,
   Then each take a pin
And pick lint from the other one's navel.

* * *

Big Bertha got flabby from beer,
So enormously large that, oh, dear,
   Once far out in the ocean,
   She made such a commotion
That the Russians torpedoed her rear.

Macho Musings

Sy once met an actress named Ruth
In a cocktail lounge telephone booth.
   Now he knows the perfection
    Of an ideal connection
Even if somewhat uncouth!

* * *

A mathematician named Paul
Has a hexahedronical ball,
   And the square of its weight
   Times his pecker, plus eight,
Is his phone number—give him a call.

* * *

"Lady," said Michael DeFore,
"I can't go on anymore.
   I'm all in a sweat,
   And you haven't come yet,
And it's nearly a quarter past four."

"Mike," came a voice from the bed.
"Such complaints are surely ill bred.
   Your pecker's so small,
   There's no friction at all
To bring my desires to a head."

* * *

In the interest of furthering vice,
Proposition all chicks at least twice.
   They may come out scrapping
   At first and start slapping,
But the second attempt may prove nice!

* * *

A lusty sharp stud named John Feeney
Poured a small drop of gin on his weenie.
   Then he tried to act couth,
   So he added vermouth
And slipped his girlfriend a martini.

* * *

Said Mel to his date, "Listen, Bunny,
Your crack about cash isn't funny!
   Some boffing is nice,
   But selling it's vice,
So don't dare you again mention money!"

* * *

A young castle-protecting alarmer
Was lovingly fondling his charmer.
  Said the maiden demure,
  "This is pleasant, I'm sure,
But why don't you take off your armor?"

* * *

A big chief Montana Paiute
Once had seven warts on his root.
  He poured acid on these,
  And now when he pees,
He holds the damn thing like a flute.

* * *

There was a tall cowboy from Dallas
Who enjoyed doing things with his phallus.
  So many tricks did he try
  It became, by and by,
Little more than a leather-tough callous.

* * *

There was an old cowhand named Price
Who dabbled in all sorts of vice.
  He had virgins and boys
  And mechanical toys,
And on Sundays he meddled with mice!

* * *

A Polack attending night school
Discovered red spots on his tool.
  Said the doctor, a cynic,
  "Get out of my clinic!
And wipe off the lipstick, you fool!"

* * *

A Queens dude, quite free with his dong,
Said the thing could be had for a song.
  Such response did he get
  That he rented the Met
And held auditions all the day long.

* * *

There was a smart stud name of Fink
Who possessed a very tart dink.
  To sweeten it some,
  He steeped it in rum,
And he's driven the ladies to drink.

* * *

There was a mad wrestler named Wyatt
Who kept a big girl on the quiet.
   But down on the wharf
   He kept also a dwarf
In case he should go on a diet.

* * *

There was a book salesman named Gant
Whose conduct was gay and gallant,
   For he screwed all his dozens
   Of nieces and cousins,
In addition, of course, to his aunt.

* * *

There was a mean Buffalo dude
Whose mind was excessively lewd.
   He asserted, ''All women
    Seen dancin' or swimmin'
Would rather be home gettin' screwed.''

* * *

A lumberjack from Klamath Falls
Whose subscriptions to *Vogue* and *McCall's*,
   Inflamed such a passion
    For feminine fashion
That he knitted a snood for his balls.

* * *

There was a nice naval cadet
Whose dreams were unusually wet.
   When he dreamt of his wedding,
    He soaked up the bedding,
And the wedding ain't taken place yet.

* * *

The new women's styles are first-class
For revealing a shapely young lass.
　　But though better to view her,
　　It's tougher to screw her
With her stockings up over her ass.

* * *

Lin Fong was a horny Chinese
Who unhappily caught a disease.
　　So he dipped his penie
　　In a double martini;
Now he screws with the greatest of ease.

* * *

A Wyoming herder named Sloate
Fell in love with a young nanny goat.
　　The daughter he sired
　　Was greatly admired
For her beautiful angora coat.

* * *

There was a young Pole name of "Ski"
Whose knowledge of French was "Oui, Oui."
  When they said, *"Parlez vous?"*
  He replied, "Same as you."
He was famed for his bright repartee!

* * *

Young Peter, with passions quite gingery,
Tore a hole in his sister's best lingerie.
  He pinched her behind,
  Then made up his mind
To add incest to insult and injury.

* * *

High up in an elm in the park,
He climbed with his sweetie to spark.
  At last, in a passion,
  They did it dog fashion;
Oh, you should've seen that tree bark!

* * *

There's a Polack who's from San Berdoo,
And he bites all his oysters in two.
  But he has certain misgivings
  That some might be living
Who would kick up one hullabaloo.

* * *

A Sergeant of troop personnel
Said: "G.I.s can all go to hell.
   What they do to my wife
   Is the curse of life —
And, God blast them, they do it so well!"

* * *

Big Sam has won several prizes
With balls that are different sizes.
   His tool, when at ease,
   Reaches down to his knees;
Oh, what it must be when it rises!

* * *

A Volkswagen owner named Clete
Once dated a nympho in heat.
   She gave so much action,
   She put him in traction,
And he cried, "What a screwy back seat!"

* * *

A cowboy from Old Santa Fe
Seemed to women the ultimate lay.
  His machismo was such
  Girls swooned at his touch,
But to tell you the truth, he was gay.

* * *

There was an old rich Japanese
Who said to the girl on his knees,
  "You would heighten my bliss
  If you played more with this
And paid less attention to these."

* * *

They say a cow rancher named Hutton
Had a penchant for all forms of mutton.
  Be it ewe, lamb, or ram,
  He gave not a damn
But straightway began to unbutton.

* * *

When it comes to a nice-a big behind
If you try-a some samples you find
   That-a pinch and-a feel
    Will make-a da girl squeal,
But atsa something she no really mind.

* * *

An Oregon logger named Patchett
Lopped off his love log with a hatchet,
   Then sent it by mailer
    To Morris, the tailor,
Who made him a small snatch to match it.

* * *

The last time I dined with the King
He did quite a curious thing.
   He sat on a stool
   And took out his tool,
And said, "If I play, will you sing?"

* * *

A Tampa shoe salesman named Curt
Was attracted by every new skirt.
   Oh, it wasn't their minds
   But their rounded behinds
That excited this lovable flirt.

45

* * *

Expressing surprise at her shyness,
The butler remarked to her Highness,
  "You'll find beyond doubt
  When my snake is stretched out
It'll reach damn near up to your sinus!"

* * *

There was a pipe fitter in Boise
Who at times was exceedingly noise;
  So his friends' joy increased
  When he moved way back East
To what people in Brooklyn call Joise.

* * *

A gay politician named Dean
Was caught frolicking in the latrine,
  He claimed it was rape,
  But they have it on tape,
And his smile's positively obscene.

* * *

A Myrtle Beach lifeguard named Dan
Likes to grind a gal's rind on the sand.
   When gnats are about,
   He'll not take it out,
Which accounts for the bites on his can.

* * *

In Brownsville, a cowboy named Tex
Has fun swatting flies with his sex.
   Those knowing its length
   And inordinate strength
Say it gives flies disastrous effects.

* * *

A vasectomy, that's what I'll get!
Then shacking will be a sure bet.
   I'll promise quite firm
   No issues of sperm
And never a late-monthly sweat!

"I love ya, my lovely Virginia,
I'm dyin' to wed ya, to win ya.
　　But if you say, 'No!'
　　At least grant this schmo
The pleasure of puttin' it in ya!"

* * *

In the Garden of Eden lay Adam,
Stroking the charms of his madam;
　　And he chuckled with mirth,
　　For he knew that on earth
'Twas but one set of tools, and he had 'em!

Femme Funnies

A pretty young "stewie" named Myrtle
Had quite an affair with a turtle.
   And what's more phenomenal,
   A swelling abdominal
Proved to Myrtle the turtle was fertile.

* * *

A baker from Pittsburgh named Shaker
Once deflowered a pretty young Quaker.
   And when he had done it,
   She straightened her bonnet
And said, "I give thanks to my maker."

* * *

An actress who lives in New York
Is quite cautious from fear of the stork.
   You will find she is taped
   To prevent being raped,
And her rectum is plugged with a cork.

* * *

While dancing a fast minuet,
A spinster became quite upset
   When her partner in dance
   Burst the fly in his pants
And his tool twirled a brisk pirouette.

* * *

A true baseball fan named Miss Glend
Was the Dodgers' best rooter and friend;
   But for her the big league
   Never held the intrigue
Of a bat with two balls at the end.

* * *

There was a great redhead from Lithem
Who sang with a band and slept with 'em.
   It's sad to relate
   She's borne twelve kids to date,
Six brass, four reeds, and two rhythm.

* * *

There was a smart waitress in Reno
Who lost all her dough playing Keno;
   But she lay on her back,
   Exposing her crack,
And now she owns the casino.

* * *

When Godiva rode out on her horse, oh,
How much she displayed of her torso!
   A crowd soon collected;
   The ladies objected,
But men cried, "We'd love to see more so!"

There was a Bronx hooker named Bunny
Whose kisses were sweeter than honey;
　　Her callers galore
　　Would line up at her door
To take turns in paying her money.

　　　　　* * *

There was a pert prostie with pride
Whose doctor cut open her hide.
　　He misplaced his stitches
　　And closed the wrong niches;
She now does her work on the side.

* * *

A Miami swinger named Cookie
Said, "I like to mix gambling with nookie.
  Before every race,
  I go home to my place
And curl up with a very good bookie."

* * *

She wasn't what one would call pretty,
And other girls offered her pity;
  But nobody guessed
  That her Wassermann test
Involved half the men of the city.

* * *

A homely old spinster named Dunn
Wed a short-peckered son-of-a-gun.
  She said, "I don't care
  If there isn't much there.
God knows it is better than none."

* * *

There was a sweet farm girl from Worcester
Who dreamt that a rooster seduced her.
  She woke with a scream
  But 'twas only a dream—
A bump in the mattress had goosed her.

* * *

"I'd like you to kiss me," she said.
"Between my toes, please bend your head.
  Not there, Oh, no, no!
  It tickles me so;
Between the two big ones, instead!"

* * *

A carnal old bag in Pomona
Just wearing a flowered kimona,
  In a manner psychotic
  And autoerotic,
Jabs herself with a stick of bologna.

* * *

Said a Polish feminist named Cox,
"I on birth control pills wish a pox.
  Some find them divine,
  But when I'm using mine,
They always fall out of my box."

* * *

A ravishing French mademoiselle
Walked down the docks ringing a bell.
  When asked why she rang it,
  She answered, "God damn it,
To ze sailors I've zomething to sell."

* * *

"My fantasy," sighed Miss Van Dyke,
"Is to sin with a lez that I like!
  To part her sweet beaver
  And then to relieve her
With my battery-powered spike."

* * *

There was a slick chick very sweet
Who thought sailors' meat quite a treat.
   When she sat on their lap,
   She unbuttoned their flap
And always had plenty to eat.

* * *

A women's lib leader named Klutz
Is known to have plenty of guts.
   When asked what she'd need
   To be totally freed,
She snarled at the reporter, "Nuts!"

* * *

There once was a little girl scout
Who found herself troubled by doubt.
   "If that's only a finger,"
   She said, "it may linger.
But otherwise take it right out."

* * *

There was a young Tulsan named Riddle
Whose girl had to teach him to fiddle.
　　She grabbed hold of his bow
　　And said, "If you want to know,
You can try parting my hair in the middle."

* * *

Said Cynthia on one of her larks,
"It's nicer in bed than in parks.
　　You feel more at ease,
　　Your fanny don't freeze,
And crude passers don't make snide remarks."

* * *

A dollie from Denver named Jill
Each evening would swallow a pill.
　　And when she conceived,
　　So great was she grieved,
She sued the drug store for a mil.

* * *

Said a Boston blonde big-busted siren,
"Young sailors are cute, I must try one!"
    She came home in the nude,
    Stewed, screwed, and tattooed,
With lewd pictures and poems by Byron.

* * *

A buxom Bronx waitress named Mandy
Had a pair that really was dandy.
   She would give the right one
   To her new baby son
And the left to whoever was handy.

* * *

A dizzy young damsel who dreamed
She was out in a boat being reamed
   By a snake in a lake
   Mused aloud, when awake,
"It can't be as nice as it seemed!"

* * *

Said an oversexed actress named Lou,
Who admitted to age forty-two,
   "I just love this sweet, precious
   Menopause that refreshes.
Now I don't give a damn what I do!"

* * *

There was a cute nympho named Maude,
And she was a terrible fraud.
   To screw at the table,
   She never was able,
But out in the kitchen—Oh, Lawd!

* * *

A sensuous Indian Sioux
Once asked her chief, "What shall I dioux?"
   So they went to her tepee;
   She then looked in her peepee
And said, "I'm not sleepee. Let's scrioux!"

* * *

No matter how Gail exercises
Her boobies are of different sizes.
   The one that is small
   Is of no use at all,
But the other's won several prizes.

To Tessie, the touch of a male meant
An emotional cardiac ailment.
  And acuteness of breath
  Caused her untimely death
In the course of erotic impalement.

* * *

There was an old waitress named Pager
Who, as a result of a wager,
  Consented to fart
  The whole oboe part
Of Mozart's Quartet in F Major.

* * *

In Rome, sighed Gina Marie Zimcucia,
"I'm sick an' a tired wit' da push-a
   When I lie on my back
   An' you fill-a da' crack
An' I gotta get uppa and dush-a!"

* * *

Said a seductive filly in heat,
"To me a good lay is a treat!
   I have an addiction
   To pleasurable friction,
Like the motion of meat rubbing meat!"

* * *

Said an erotic carnal young teacher
   named Polly,
"I'm told loving schoolboys is folly.
   If those who decry it
   Would give in and try it,
They'd find it is perfectly jolly!"

* * *

It's easy to be full of glee
When your bra is a 42-D;
  But the gal worthwhile
  Is the gal who can smile
With two bosoms the size of a pea.

* * *

Said the wench to the new maharajah,
"Oh, you're really well hung, you old codjah!
  I'm delighted to lay
  And be queen for a day,
But the last maharajah was largah!"

* * *

A luscious young nymph named Dorella
Was raped by an ape in a cella'.
  She cried, "That baboon
  Went and came too damn soon,
But then so does the average fella!"

* * *

What a wicked young Jane is Miss Thayer;
She's a dope pusher and a horse player.
  And something else, too,
  For each time you screw,
She always insists that you pay her.

* * *

A cute plumber known as "The Greek"
Was called in by a dame with a leak.
  She looked so becoming,
  He fixed all her plumbing
And didn't emerge for a week.

* * *

A waitress from old Monterey
Was asked to make love in the hay.
  She jumped at the chance
  But held on to her pants,
For she never had tried it that way!

* * *

Sweet Gwen joined the boys at a smoker,
Then lost her first game of strip poker.
  She gave birth to the pot
  In nine months on the dot
And cried, "Now I'm discarding the joker!"

On Betty's white bosom there leaned
The jaw of a mad Brooklyn fiend;
   But she pulled up his head
   And sarcastically said,
"For God's sake, won't you ever be weaned?"

* * *

A show girl in Vegas named Jo
Went down on every Tom, Dick, and Bo.
   When it came to a test,
   She was voted the best,
And practice makes perfect, you know.

* * *

Nymphomaniacal Alice
Used a dynamite stick for a phallus.
  They found her vagina
  In South Carolina
And her fanny in Fontainebleau Palace.

* * *

One night Bobbi had an affair
With a fellow all covered with hair.
  Then she picked up his hat
  And realized that
She'd been diddled by Smokey the Bear.

* * *

There was a prim spinster whose joys
Were achieved with incomparable poise.
  She could have an orgasm
  With never a spasm
And could fart without making a noise.

An Amazon scantily clad
Was wooed by a primitive lad.
　　She said, "Tho' you dig me,
　　My God! You're a pigmy.
That's the smallest *putz* I've ever had!"

* * *

A famed fellatrice named Tess
Turned down all requests from the press.
　　To explain her renown
　　As a great goer down,
She was tight-lipped about her success.

Clerical Clowning

The bashful Reverend Geary
Of girls was exceedingly leery.
  Then the organist Pru
  Showed him how and with who
He could render his evenings more cheery.

* * *

There was a cute typist named Devon
Who was raped in the garden by seven
  High Anglican priests,
  The lascivious beasts.
Of such is the Kingdom of Heaven.

* * *

A preacher whose sight was myopic
Thought sex an incredible topic.
  So poor were his eyes
  That despite its great size,
His penis appeared microscopic.

* * *

The book of God's beneath you;
The Man of God's above you.
  Salvation pole
  Is in your hole;
Now wiggle your ass to save your soul!

* * *

A friar of peculiar intent
Gave up pederasty for Lent;
   But just to make sure
   His resolve remained pure,
He pounded a cork in his vent.

* * *

The dong of a preacher named Randall
Shot sparks like a big Roman candle.
   He was much in demand,
   For the colors were grand,
But the girls found him too hot to handle.

* * *

A lecherous curate of Leeds
Was discovered one day in the weeds.
   Astride a young nun,
   He said, "Christ, this is fun—
Far better than telling one's beads."

* * *

A careless choir leader named Drew
Led songs with his garments askew.
   Some dames in the flock
   Eyed the organ with shock,
While others passed out in their pew.

* * *

There was a chic Spanish contessa,
A rather unblushing transgressor.
  When sent to the priest,
  The lewd little beast
Began to undress her confessor.

* * *

A lecherous priest named Fitzhugh
Screwed a parishioner's wife in a pew.
  "I'll admit I'm not pious,"
  He said, "I've a bias.
I think it diviner to screw."

* * *

An oversexed cleric named Clay
Kept his wife in the family way
  Till she grew more alert,
  Bought a vaginal squirt,
And said to her spouse, "Let us spray!"

* * *

Years back a young parson named Parrage
Tried to grind his betrothed in a carriage.
   She said, "No, you young goose,
   Just try self-abuse,
And the other we'll try after marriage."

* * *

The girls in the Rose Bowl Parade
Raised the rod of young Father McDade.
   Hard up for some fun,
   He went home on the run
And diddled his grandmother's maid.

* * *

When Paul the Apostle lay prostrate
And leisurely prodded his prostate,
   With pride parabolic,
   His most apostolic
Appendage became an apostate.

There was an old monk named O'Shea
Who of fasting grew tired every day.
    Till at length with a yell,
    He burst from his cell.
"From now on I'm going to be gay."

* * *

There was a bold actress named Alice
Who peed in a Catholic chalice.
    The padre agreed
    'Twas done out of need
And not out of Protestant malice.

* * *

The sweet spinster lady Miss Sue
Was dozing one day in her pew.
   When the preacher cried, "Sin!"
   She replied, "Count me in
Just as soon as the preachin' is through!"

* * *

There was a sweet nanny from Tottenham
Whose manners, well, she'd forgotten 'em.
   While at tea at the vicar's,
   She kicked off her knickers,
Explaining she felt much too hot in 'em.

* * *

A Mexican nun, Sister Donna,
Was hot as a day in Tijuana;
   But when the old bishop
   Could not get his fish up,
She said, "Anyhow, I don' wanna."

* * *

The Reverend Henry Ward Beecher
Called a girl a most elegant creature.
  So she laid on her back
  And exposing her crack
Said, "Screw that, you old Sunday school
    teacher!"

* * *

There was a dear priest named Delaney
Who said to the girls, *"Nota bene.*
  I've seen how you swish up
  Your skirts at the bishop
Whenever the weather is rainy."

* * *

As His Eminence signed my petition
He said, "I take this position:
  Here shines a clean mind,
  For nowhere can I find
A single lubricious omission!"

* * *

A Los Angeles churchman named Cheyney
Made love to a spinster named Janie.
  When his friends said, "Oh, dear,
  She's so old and so queer,"
He replied, "But the day was so rainy!"

* * *

There was an old priest named McClore
Whose tool was a yard long or more,
  So he wore the damn thing
  In a surgical sling
To keep it from wiping the floor.

* * *

A warmhearted priest named McCall
Consistently practiced withdrawal.
  This quaint predilection
  Created such friction,
He soon had no foreskin at all.

* * *

There was a Maine cleric named Meyer
Who was seized with a carnal desire.
  And his passionate snorts
  Were the parish priest's shorts
That hung up to dry by the fire.

God's plan made a hopeful beginning,
But Man spoiled his chances by sinning.
　　We trust that the story
　　Will end in God's glory,
But at present the other side's winning.

There was a young sexton named Syngs
Who talked about God and such things;
　　But his secret desire
　　Was a boy in the choir
With a bottom like jelly on springs.

A pastor predicting man's doom
Was exceedingly fond of the womb.
　　He thought nothing finer
　　Than the human vagina,
So he kept three or four in his room.

* * *

There once was an old Irish priest
Who lived almost fully on yeast;
    For he said, "It is plain
    We must all rise again,
And I want to get started at least."

* * *

From the depths of the crypt at St. Styles
Came a scream that resounded for miles.
    Said the vicar, "Good gracious!
    Has Father Ignatius
Forgotten the bishop has piles?"

* * *

There once was a boring old priest
Whose sermons one felt never ceased.
    His hearers, en masse,
    Got fatigued to the ass
And slept through the most sacred feast.

There was once a Father O'Neil
Who wondered just how it would feel
  To carry a gong
  Hanging down from his dong
And occasionally let the thing peal.

So he rigged up a clever device
And tried the thing out once or twice;
  But it wasn't the gong
  But rather his prong
That peeled, and it didn't feel nice!

* * *

There was an old maid in a pew
Who said as the curate withdrew:
  "I prefer the dear vicar;
  He's longer and thicker;
Besides, he comes quicker than you."

* * *

There was a bold lady of Twickenham
Who regretted some men had no prick in 'em.
  On her knees every day,
  To God she would pray
To lengthen and strengthen and thicken 'em.

* * *

There was a gay monk of Siberia
Who of frigging grew weary and wearier.
  At last, with a yell,
  He burst from his cell
And buggered the Father Superior.

There once was a clergyman's daughter
Who detested all boy friends who sought her
  Till she found one whose dong
  Was as hard and as long
As the prayers that her father had taught her.

* * *

A born-again Christian named Claire
Was having her first love affair.
  As she climbed into bed,
  She reverently said,
"I wish to be opened with prayer."

Global Giggles

A publisher once went to France
In search of a tale of romance.
  A Parisian lady
  Told a story so shady
That the publisher made an advance.

* * *

There was an artiste from Montmartre
Who was famed far and wide for his fart.
 When they said, "What a noise!"
 He replied with great poise,
"When I fart, wee, I fart from ze heart."

* * *

A pathetic old maid of Bordeaux
Fell in love with a dashing young beau.
 To arrest his regard,
 She would squat in his yard
And appealingly pee in the snow.

* * *

There was an Italian cadet,
And this is the damndest thing yet.
 His tool was so long
 And incredibly strong,
He could bugger six Greeks *en brochette*.

* * *

A bold violinist in Rio
Was seducing a lady named Cleo.
  As she took down her panties,
  She said, "No *andantes;*
I want this *allegro con brio!*"

* * *

A tea grower straight from Darjeeling
Whose dong reaches up to the ceiling
  Plugs into a socket
  To rock it and shock it.
Oh, God! What a wonderful feeling!

* * *

The beautiful princess of Siam
Once said to her lover, young Kiam,
  "If you screw me, of course,
  You will have to use force,
But God knows you're stronger than I am."

* * *

A Korean whose home was in Seoul
Had notions uncommonly droll;
   He'd get himself stewed
   And pose in the nude
On top of a telephone pole.

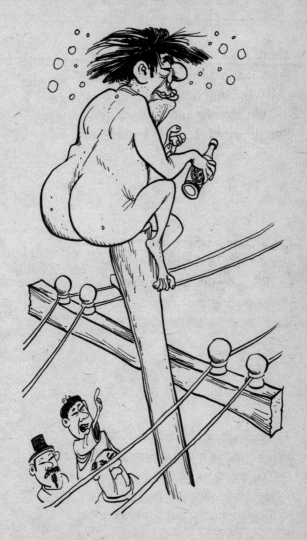

* * *

There was a teen tart in Madrid
Who learned she was having a kid.
   By holding her water
   Two months and a quarter,
She drowned the poor bastard, she did.

* * *

On a picnic a Scot named McGee
Was stung in the balls by a bee.
   He made oodles of money
   By oozing pure honey
Each time he attempted to pee.

* * *

There was an old impotent Scot
Who enticed a young girl on his yacht.
   Too aged to rape her,
   He made darts of paper,
Which he lazily threw at her twat.

* * *

There was a slick dude man from Liberia
Who was groping a wench from Nigeria.
  He said, "Say, my pet,
  Your panties are wet."
"Sorry, sir, that's my interior."

* * *

Said a beautiful whore of Hong Kong
To a long-pronged patron named Wong,
  "They say my vagina's
  The nicest in China.
Don't ruin it by donging it wrong."

* * *

A thrifty old Scotsman named Ewing
Inquired, "Why be bothered with screwing?
  It's safer and cleaner
  To finger your weiner,
And besides you can see what you're doing."

* * *

Despite her impressive physique,
Salome was really quite meek.
  If a mouse showed its head,
  She would jump into bed
With a terrible blood-curdling shiek.

* * *

Once a bold eunuch of Roylem
Took eggs to the cook and said, "Boil 'em.
  I'll sling 'em beneath
  My inadequate sheath
And slip into the harem and foil 'em."

* * *

There once was a fellow from Sydney
Who put it in up to her kidney;
   But a guy from Quebec
   Put it up to her neck.
Now he had a giant one, didn't he?

* * *

A maid in the land of Aloha
Was determined that no one should know her.
   One brash tourist tried,
   But she wiggled aside
And spilled all the spermatozoa.

* * *

Said the sharp-eyed Chinese detective,
"Can it be that my eyesight's defective?
   Has your east tit the least bit
   The best of the west tit?
Or is it a trick of perspective?"

* * *

In La France once a clevair dear man
Met a girl on the beach down at Cannes.
    Said the mademoiselle,
    "Eh, m'sieu, vot ze'ell?
Stay away where eet ees not sun tan!"

* * *

A ravishing tart in Pompeii
Used to make ninety lire per lay;
    But age dimmed her renown,
    And now she lies down
Fifty times for the same pay.

* * *

A prostie that sailors thought sweet
Was hawking her meat in the street.
    While ambling one day
    In a casual way,
She clapped up the whole British fleet.

* * *

There was an old count of Swoboda
Who'd not pay a whore what he owed her.
  So with great savoir-faire
  She stood on a chair
And pissed in his whiskey and soda.

* * *

There once was a midwife of Gaul
Who had hardly no business at all.
  She cried, "Hell and damnation!
  There's no procreation.
God made the French penis too small."

* * *

There once was a handsome young Haitian,
The luckiest dog in creation.
  He worked for the rubber trust
  Teaching the upper crust
The science of safe copulation.

* * *

Once a great salesman of Leeds
Rashly swallowed six packets of seeds.
  In a month, silly ass,
  He was covered with grass,
And he couldn't sit down for the weeds.

* * *

There was a smart German named Fritz
Who planted an acre of tits.
   They came up in the fall,
   Pink nipples and all,
And he chewed them all up into bits.

* * *

A remarkable race are the Persians;
They have such peculiar diversions.
   They make love all day
   In the regular way
And save up the nights for perversions.

* * *

Thus spoke the king of Siam,
"For women, I don't give a damn;
   But a fat-bottomed boy
   Is my pride and my joy.
They call me a bugger, I am."

* * *

A whimsical Arab from Aden,
His masculine member well laden,
   Cried: "Nuptial joy,
   When shared with a boy,
Is better than melon or maiden!"

* * *

There was a young man of Bengal
Who swore he had only one ball.
   Then two little bitches
   Just pulled down his britches
And found that he had none at all.

* * *

Kukai was a shy Japanese
Who handled his tool with great ease.
   This continual friction
   Made his sex a mere fiction,
But the callous hangs down to his knees.

* * *

There was a young sailor from Brighton
Who remarked to his date, "You're a tight
    one."
  She remarked, "Bless my soul,
  You're in the wrong hole;
There's plenty of room in the right one."

* * *

An old spinster born in Vancouver
Once captured a man by maneuver.
  She jumped on his tool,
  Then laughed like a fool,
And nothing on earth could remove her.

* * *

There was a sweet *fraulein* from Munich
Who was had in a park by a eunuch.
  In a moment of passion,
  He shot her a ration
From a squirt gun concealed 'neath his tunic.

* * *

Near the barracks there lives a young lass
Who is said to have two breasts of brass.
  A soldier who bit her
  Found in one a transmitter,
For she works for the news house of Tass!

* * *

There once lived a Roman named Nero
Who in bed was not much of a hero.
  When invited to diddle,
  He'd come with his fiddle,
So his score with the ladies was zero!

* * *

Said a Hindi in heat in Bombay,
"I've prayed for a lay the whole day!
  Now I'll have one, I vow,
  With the first sacred cow
That looks gentle and gets in my way!"

* * *

Said a cute mademoiselle in Paree,
"It cost you fifty bucks to lay me.
  I do it French way
  For ze double of pay,
But ze fashion of dogs I do free!"

* * *

There was a tough gal of Ostend
Who swore she'd hold out to the end;
  But alas! halfway over,
  'Twixt Calais and Dover,
She done what she didn't intend.

There was a meek chap of Cape Horn
Who wished he had never been born.
   And he wouldn't have been
   If his father had seen
That the end of the rubber was torn.

* * *

A fantastic rich prince of Sirocco
Had erotical penchants rococo.
   The prong of this prince
   Was flavored with quince,
And he seasoned his semen with cocoa.

* * *

There was an old fag in Madrid
Who cast loving eyes on a kid.
   He said, "Oh, my joy!
   I'll bugger that boy.
You see if I don't," and he did.

A lesbian once in Khartoum
Asked a fairy up to her room;
  They spent the whole night
  In a hell of a fight
As to which should do what and to whom.

* * *

There was a neat babe from Hong Kong
Whose cervical cap was a gong.
  She said with a yell
  As a shot rang the bell,
"I'll give you a ding for a dong."

* * *

A bobby of Nottingham Junction
Whose organ had long ceased to function
   Deceived his good wife
   For the rest of her life
With the aid of his constable's truncheon.

* * *

There was a tall *Herr* in Berlin
Whose tool was the size of a pin.
   Said his girl with a laugh
   As she fondled his shaft,
"Well, this won't be much of a sin."

* * *

There was a hot Hindu of Jaipur
Who fell madly in love with a viper.
   With screams of delight,
   He'd retire each night
With the viper concealed in his diaper.

* * *

Every time Lady Smythington swoons,
Her boobies pop out like balloons.
   But her butler stands by
   With hauteur in his eye
And puts them back gently with spoons!

* * *

An amorous cowboy from Rio
Once met a young lady named Cleo.
　A full night and a day
　They spent in the hay,
And now the poor cowboy can't pee-o.

* * *

Said Queen Isabella of Spain,
"I'd like it just now and again.
　But please let me explain
　That by now and again,
I mean *now* and again and again."

* * *

A scholar from England named Adam
Took a pot shot at splitting the atom.
　He blew off his penis,
　And now, just between us,
He's known throughout Britain as madam.

* * *

There was a grand stud from Peru
Who was hard up for something to do,
    So he took out his carrot
    And buggered his parrot
And sent the results to the zoo.

* * *

A schoolgirl from Brighton named Tillie
Had a craving to walk Piccadilly.
    She said: "Ain't it funny?
    It ain't for the money!
But if I don't take it, it's silly."

* * *

There was a spry Frenchman from Gaul
Who went to a fancy-dress ball.
    Just for a whim,
    He dressed up as a quim
And was had by the dog in the hall.

* * *

There was a *senôr* in Havana
Banged his girl on the player piana.
  At the height of their fever,
  Her rear hit the lever,
And "Yes, he now has no banana!"

* * *

There was a young sweet Scottish lass
Who had a magnificent ass;
  Not rounded and pink,
  As you probably think,
It was gray, had long ears, and ate grass.

Campus Cuties

There was a cool coed named Florence
Who for kissing professed great abhorrence;
   But when she'd been kissed
   And found what she'd missed,
She cried till the tears came in torrents.

* * *

There was a keen coed named White
Who got drunk with a Phi Ep one night.
  She came to in bed
  With a split maidenhead;
That's the last time she ever was tight.

* * *

At Rutgers, a coed named Trapper
In psychology class was a napper.
  But her Freudian dreams
  Were so classic, it seems,
That now she's a Phi Beta Kappa.

* * *

A Liberal Arts major at Swarthmore
Had a date with a sexy young sophomore.
  As quick as a glance,
  He stripped off his pants,
But he found that the sophomore'd got off
    more.

* * *

A coed with features cherubic
Was famed for her area pubic.
   When they asked her its size,
   She replied in surprise,
"Are you speaking of square feet or cubic?"

* * *

There was a good student at Yale
Whose face was exceedingly pale.
   He spent his vacation
   In self-masturbation
Because of the high price of tail.

* * *

There was a shy coed named Sue
Who preferred a stiff drink to a screw;
   But one leads to the other,
   And now she's a mother:
Let this be a lesson to you.

* * *

There was a soph named Hortense
The size of whose boobs were immense.
  One day playing soccer
  Out popped her left knocker,
And she kicked it right over the fence.

* * *

A botany major called Sis
Simply thought it the apex of bliss
   To jazz herself silly
   With the bud of a lily,
Then go to the garden and piss.

* * *

There was a Brown coed named Rose
Who could diddle herself with her toes.
   She did it so neat,
   She fell in love with her feet
And christened them Jethro and Mose.

* * *

A psychotic rich kid from Tulane
Caused his mother considerable pain.
   He poured nitroglycerin
   Where his dad put his pisser in
And then threw her right under a train.

* * *

At Radcliffe sex isn't injurious,
Though of love we are never penurious.
  Thanks to vulcanized aids,
  Though we die as old maids,
At least we shall never die curious.

* * *

A pert Kansas coed named Smith
Whose virtue was largely a myth
  Said: "Try as I can
  I can't find a man
Whom it's fun to be virtuous with."

* * *

A Vassar girl loves not her lover
So much as she loves his love of her.
  Then loves she her lover,
  For love of her lover,
Or love of her love of her lover?

There was a New Yorker named Nance
Who attended a debutante dance.
  She inspected the cellar
  With an Ivy League feller,
And now all her sisters are aunts.

* * *

A lusty sophomore from Savannah
Once screwed herself good with banana.
  Then she went off to Macon,
  Greased her fanny with bacon,
And slid on it into Atlanta.

A winsome young rushee named Randall
Once caused a sorority scandal
   By coming out bare
   On the main campus square
And frigging herself with a candle.

* * *

A Maryland soph I'm not namin'
Asked a coed he thought he was tamin',
   "Have you your maidenhead?"
   "Don't be foolish," she said,
"But I still have the box that it came in."

* * *

A virgin young preppy named Alice
Had thought of her sheath as a chalice.
   One night sleeping nude,
   She awoke feeling lewd
And found in her chalice a phallus.

* * *

A USC coed named Stark
Will fool around just in the dark.
　　She coos, "It's not right
　　To turn on in the light,
So turn off the headlights and park!"

* * *

There was a coy preppy Miss Patch
Who had a rectangular hatch;
　　She practiced coition
　　With a mathematician
Who had a fine square root to match.

* * *

A Princeton professor named Ted
Dreamed one night of a buxom coed.
　　He mussed her and bussed her
　　And then quickly fussed her,
But the action was all in his head.

* * *

A coed who was built mighty trimly
Once reproached for not acting more primly
   Answered: "Heavens above,
   I know sex is not love,
But what a terrific facsim'le!"

* * *

A perky Cal coed named Kay
Would not let men have their own way;
   But one night in the park,
   She was had by a narc.
Now she goes to the park every day.

* * *

A Kent State coed in Rangoon
Was screwed once by a hairy baboon.
   "Well, it has been great fun,"
   She remarked when he'd done,
"But I'm sorry you came quite so soon."

* * *

There was a cute coed named Jane
Who declared she'd a man on the brain;
   But you knew from the view
   Of her waist as it grew,
It was not on her brain that he'd lain.

* * *

There was a nice girl from Penn State
Who stuttered when out on a date.
By the time she cried, "S-s-s-stop!"
Or called for a c-c-c-cop,
It was often a wee bit too late.

* * *

Up in Cambridge, Lib Cliffies discard
Any pretense of being on guard.
Though the Harvards deny it,
Their saltpeter diet
Makes it hard to get hard in the Yard.

* * *

A Florida nympho named Prudence
Spent the night in a frat house with students.
By the dawn's early light,
She slipped out of sight,
And she left not a single protuberance!

* * *

A fullback at Purdue named Jones
Has reduced many coeds to moans
  By his wonderful knowledge
  Found out while in college
Of women's most sensual zones.

* * *

The Tri Delt knew nothing of mergin',
And her sisters all thought her a virgin
  Till they found her in bed
  With her quim very red
And the head of a kid just emergin'.

* * *

There was a housemother named Rose
Who'd occasionally straddle a hose
  And parade about, squirting
  And spouting and spurting,
Pretending she pissed like her beaux.

"Far dearer to me than all treasure,"
A Cliffie once said, "is my leisure,
   For then I can screw
   The whole Harvard crew.
They're slow, but it lengthens the pleasure."

* * *

So well stacked the freshman named Brenda
That profs yearned to part her pudenda.
   So they were quite irate
   When her first campus date
Wasn't Moe, Jack, or Manny but Glenda.

* * *

A Michigan coed named Mabel
Once said, "I don't think that I'm able;
   But I'm willing to try,
   So where shall I lie?
On the bed, on the floor, or the table?"

* * *

A cute Cliffie who loved her Supp-hose,
Had erogenous zones in her toes.
   She remained onanistic
   Till a foot fetishistic
Young prof became one of her beaus.

* * *

There was a coed from Bryn Mawr
Who'd lie on a mat on the floor;
   In a manner uncanny,
   She'd wiggle her fanny
And drain your nuts dry to the core.

* * *

There was a sweet coed from Dover
Whose passion was such that it drove her
    To cry when you came,
    "Oh, dear! What a shame!
Well, now we shall have to start over!"

* * *

There was a frosh fullback from Wooster
Who thought of himself as a rooster.
    If he saw a fine chick,
    He had just one trick;
He goosed her, seduced, and dejuiced her.

* * *

Sighed a prudish young coed from Trinity,
"Thank God, I've still got my virginity!
    Though I've had no men,
    I'll admit, now and then,
I have stuffed objects about that vicinity."

* * *

A Wisconsin coed with gall
Attended a fancy-dress ball.
    Some say that she wore
    Less behind than before,
While others said: "Nothing at all."

* * *

At Miami there was a sweet maid
Who swore that she wasn't afraid;
    But a sophomore named Jerry
    Came after her cherry.
'Twasn't just an advance, 'twas a raid!

* * *

They once hid a hooker at Yale
With her price list tattooed on her tail;
    And on her behind,
    For the sake of the blind,
She had it embroidered in Braille.

*   *   *

There was a cheerleader named Claire
Who knelt in the moonlight all bare.
    She prayed to her God
    For a boff on the sod,
And the football coach answered her prayer!

*   *   *

When Peggy spots a farm boy at school
In the corridor, loping his mule,
   She raises her dress,
   And you will never guess
What she tells him to do with his tool.

*   *   *

There was a Duke coed named Lynn
Who thought all lovemaking a sin;
   But when she got tight,
   It seemed quite all right,
So the seniors all plied her with gin.

*   *   *

A Brigham Young senior named Schneider
Once took out a girl just to ride her.
   She allowed him to feel
   From her neck to her heel
But never would let him inside her.

138

* * *

There was a coed to admire
Who succumbed to a fullback's desire.
   She said, "It's a sin,
   But now that it's in,
Could you shove it a few inches higher?"

* * *

There was a Cal freshman named Jenny
Who would do it for only a penny.
   She lived just to hump
   And to grind her fat rump,
A source of amusement to many.

* * *

When at college a girl cannot win,
What with studies and sex and bad gin;
   And it's just the last straw
   When the dean says, "Withdraw,"
When it's him that's been sticking it in.

* * *

A frosh whose particular vice
Was to make herself peckers of ice
   Explained, "While they're chilly
   And perhaps somewhat silly,
They cool my device very nice!"

* * *

A Rice business major named Ida
Said to Ned as he slid it insider,
   "I'd much rather be
   Underneath as 'ridee'
Than on top in the role of the rider."

* * *

"I'll tell you," smiled prom Chairman Mose,
"Why Hatty's the prom queen I chose.
   She's as cheerfully free
   As the wind on the sea,
And besides, like the wind, Hatty blows!"

* * *

There was a Drake coed called Wylde
Who kept herself quite undefiled
  By thinking of Jesus,
  Contagious diseases,
And the bother of having a child.

* * *

A coy Wellesley coed named Lizzy
Purred ''Just the thought of it makes me
    dizzy!
  It's immoral, it's vice,
  It's not at all nice,
But as long as you want it, get busy!''

* * *

Said a sexy soph from SMU
To her German professor, Hans Krew,
  ''You think reading Nietzsche
  Is perfectly peachy,
But, frankly, I'd much rather screw.''

* * *

A Hawaiian coed they call Sandal
Believed it beneath her to handle
   A young fellow's pole,
   So instead her hot hole
She contented by means of a candle.

* * *

At Wellesley, Vassar, and Smith,
A common and recurring myth
   That a masculine member
   Helps students remember
Was found without substance or pith.

Raunchy Rhythms

A widow whose singular vice
Was to keep her late husband on ice
   Said, "It's been hard since I lost him;
   I'll never defrost him!
Cold comfort but cheap at the price."

* * *

A lusty young woodsman of Maine
For years with no woman had lain,
    But he found sublimation
    At a high elevation
In the crotch of a pine. God, the pain!

* * *

A strange Portland postman named Pete
Had a very weird fetish for feet.
    One glimpse of a toe
    Would cause him to go
To an alley and finger his meat.

* * *

In Charlotte, a harlot named Sade
Was badly upset and dismayed
    By her doctor's big bill,
    Which she's paying off still,
As he knocks some off weekly in trade.

On Frisco's undergound B.A.R.T.
A swish cut a hideous fart;
   But from his sweet ass
   There will pass no more gas,
For the passengers tore him apart.

I sat next to the duchess at tea;
It was just as I feared it would be!
   Her rumblings abdominal
   Were simply phenomenal,
And everyone thought it was me!

There was a cute steno named Dru
Whose cherry a guy had got through.
   She told this to her mother,
   Who fixed her another
Out of rubber and red ink and glue.

* * *

For sculpture that's really first-class
You need form, composition, and mass.
  To do a good Venus
  Just leave off the penis
And concentrate all on the ass.

* * *

There once was a flasher named Gene
Who just loved to do things obscene.
  When women were nigh,
  He'd unbutton his fly
And shout, "Look, it's fit for the queen."

* * *

A fireman named Cuckoo Ames
Got his kicks when he played goofy games.
  He lighted the hair
  Of his lady's affair
And laughed as she peed out the flames.

* * *

There was a young wife who begat
Three husky boys, Nat, Pat, and Tat.
  They all yelled for food,
  And a problem ensued
When she found there was no tit for Tat.

* * *

When the audience hollered for more,
The ballerina couldn't encore.
  The girl had to quit
  'Cause when she did a split,
The suction stuck her to the floor.

* * *

Said a youth from Saskatchewan,
"You have something nobody can match
    you on;
  I'm referring, my dear,
  To a place at the rear
That it gives me such pleasure to pat you on."

* * *

The cross-eyed painter McNeff
Was color blind, palsied, and deaf.
  When he asked to be touted,
  The critics all shouted,
"This is art with a capital F!"

A Dallas bank watchman named Burke
Had dozed off one night during work.
  He had a wet dream
  But awoke with a scream
Just in time to give it a jerk.

* * *

Steven had a pair of pajamas
That were made from the hair of the llamas;
  But their feminine air
  Made his friends all declare
They were made from a pair of his mama's!

150

* * *

A waitress who they called "Stinky" Carter
Was widely renowned as a farter.
   Her thund'rous reports
   At Olympiad sports
Made her much in demand as a starter.

* * *

A man at a Long Island station
Had been found by a pious relation
   Making love in a ditch
   To — I won't say a bitch —
But a girl who had no reputation.

* * *

Ed slept with a tart named Marie
Who asked, "Do you fart when you pee?"
   He replied with quick art,
   "Do you pee when you fart?
If you do, then you're one up on me."

* * *

An erotic and lonely marine
Invented a funny machine,
   Concave and convex,
   It would suit either sex,
The goddamndest thing ever seen!

* * *

A Hoosier repairman named Clark
When he made love had to bark.
   His wife was a bitch
   With a terrible itch,
So Ft. Wayne can't sleep after dark!

* * *

A slightly weird fellow named Liss
Found sleep in a hearse was pure bliss.
   It does sound perverse,
   But he wished to re-hearse
His ride to the necropolis!

* * *

The insides of Tony Rozetti
Were exceedingly fragile and petty.
  All he could eat
  Was finely chopped meat,
And all he could pass was spaghetti!

* * *

A farmer who came from Okl'homa
Was awarded a special diploma
  For his telling apart
  A masculine fart
From a similar female aroma!

* * *

A hooker who ate manicotti
One night as she sat on her potty
  Contemplated with glee
  The sound of her pee
And the musical boom from her botty!

* * *

There's a Cleveland teenager named Welling,
What she does late at night she's not telling.
    She works the side streets,
    Stops the men that she meets,
And it isn't scout cookies she's selling.

A Toledo desk clerk named O'Doul
Felt his ardor grow suddenly cool.
   No lack of affection
   Reduced his erection,
But his zipper got caught on his tool.

* * *

The sea captain's tender young bride
Fell into the bay at low tide.
   You could tell by her squeals
   That some of the eels
Had discovered a dark place to hide.

* * *

On a cruise the new divorcee
Soon complained that it hurt her to pee.
   Said the handsome young mate,
   "That accounts for the fate
Of the captain, the purser, and me."

* * *

A sharpie card player, Miss Cole,
Amassed a big, horse-choking roll.
    No cards up her sleeve
    Could the suckers perceive,
For she carried her ace in the hole!

* * *

There was a cute babe from Decatur
Who was screwed by an old alligator.
    No one ever knew
    How she relished that screw,
For after he screwed her, he ate her.

* * *

The porno flick's new big emporium
Is not just a plain auditorium
    But a highly effectual,
    Heterosexual,
Mutual masturbatorium.

157

There was an old man named Calhoun
Who farted and filled a balloon,
   The balloon went so high
   That it stuck in the sky,
And stank out the Man in the Moon.

* * *

There was a Bronx model named Skinner,
Who dreamt that her lover was in her.
   She awoke with a start,
   And let out a fart,
Which was followed by luncheon and dinner.

* * *

A hillbilly boy named McGraw
Had a habit of goosing his maw.
  "Go pester your sister,"
  She said when he kissed her.
"I've trouble enough with your paw."

* * *

Said a sailor ashore in Peru,
"*Señorita, quanto por la* screw?"
  She said, "For one peso
  I will if you say so,
Con gusto, and nibble it, too!"

* * *

In Boston a man so ill bred
Once wore nothing but feathers to bed.
  Such a fetish, it's true,
  Might not suit me or you
But sure tickled the lady he spread.

* * *

You've heard of the black knight from Kent
Whose lance was so long that it bent.
   To save all the trouble,
   He put it in double,
And instead of coming, he went!

* * *

There was a pure farm girl named Grace
Who had eyes in a very odd place.
   She could sit on the hole
   Of a mouse or a mole
And stare the beast square in the face.

* * *

The bride of a brave Shawnee chief
Had a hymen in need of relief,
   So she went to the doctor
   Who prodded and shocked her
And stretched it with fingers and teeth.

* * *

A St. Louis weirdo named Will
Made his neighbors exceedingly ill
  When they learned of his habits
  Involving white rabbits
And a bird with a flexible bill.

* * *

The bouncy colleen from Dunellen,
Whom the Hoboken sailors call Helen,
  In her efforts to please
  Spread social disease
From New York to the Straits of Magellan.

* * *

There was a tall welder named Runyan
Whose pecker came down with a bunion.
  When he had an erection
  This painful infection,
Gave off a faint odor of onion.

A buggersome rancher named Reap
Remarked as he ravished a sheep,
  "I'm hoping I shall
  Someday hump a gal,
But they're neither as tight or as cheap!"

* * *

A cat house way down in Savannah
Is run in the old Southern mannah.
  The girls say, "Y'all come,"
  And the madame will strum
A banjo and hum, "Oh, Susannah."

* * *

In a bed Dee's not much of a star;
There are others more agile by far.
    But she'll spraddle out bare,
    And she'll straddle a chair,
And my gawd! What she does in a car!

* * *

Three gals and a coxswain named Jensen
Were marooned on the Isle of Ascension.
    The ladies got tough
    And swam off in a huff;
The man was the bone of contention!

* * *

A mortician's sly daughter named Maddie
Told an eager but virginal laddie,
    "If you'll do as I say,
    We can have a great lay
Since I've buried more stiffs than my
        daddy."

* * *

A tenderfoot in Tomahawk Bluff
Carried pistols to make him look tough.
   When they asked, "Do you chew?"
   He replied, "Yeth, I do,
I'm a wegular wetch of wough."

* * *

Poor Polski had no self-control;
He had an affair with a mole.
   Though bit of a nancy,
   He did like to fancy
Himself in the dominant role.

* * *

There once was a sensuous Sioux
Who liked to do nothing but scrioux;
   She would give no relief
   To her favorite chief
Until both of his balls had turned blioux.

* * *

There was an old burglar named Fife
Who found burglaring the joy of his life.
   When he entered a house
   Through the bedroom, the louse
Scared the owner half out of his wife.

* * *

A Baltimore widow named Bloom
Hung a black-ribboned wreath on her womb.
   "To remind me," she said,
   "Of my husband who's dead
And of what put him into his tomb."

* * *

There was a patrolman named Bass
Whose ballocks were made out of brass.
   When they tinkled together,
   They played "Stormy Weather,"
And lightning shot out of his ass.

* * *

A deviate groomer named Hauser
Was smitten while trimming a Schnauser.
   He lunged for the beast,
   But the mutt had a feast
When it chewed off the bone in his trouser.

Under the spreading chestnut tree,
The village smith he sat,
   Amusing himself
   By abusing himself
And catching the load in his hat.

* * *

A bank clerk who came from Winsocket
Once put a girl's hand in his pocket.
   Her delicate touch
   Thrilled his pecker so much,
It shot off in the air like a rocket.

ABOUT THE AUTHOR

This is the twenty-fourth humor collection assembled by Larry Wilde. With sales of over 6,000,000 copies, Wilde has become the largest-selling jokesmith in the history of publishing.

Mr. Wilde's literary contribution to the comedic field also includes two serious books considered to be definitive works on the subject of humor: THE GREAT COMEDIANS and HOW THE GREAT COMEDY WRITERS CREATE LAUGHTER. He has also published THE COMPLETE BOOK OF ETHNIC HUMOR, the first comprehensive assortment of jokes characterizing America's mirth-loving minorities.

Larry Wilde is a thirty-year show-business veteran, having served as a comedian, actor, writer, performer, and producer. He has appeared in the nation's finest clubs and hotels and on television in commercials as well as sitcoms.

Born in Jersey City, New Jersey, Wilde served two years in the United States Marine Corps and is a graduate of the University of Miami in Florida.

Larry lives in Los Angeles with his wife, Maryruth, where he continues to write, perform, act, and lecture on the subject of comedy. Mrs. Wilde, born in Wyoming, is the author of THE BEST OF ETHNIC HOME COOKING.

Larry Wilde

Here's how to start your own Larry Wilde
humor library!!!

____ 20811-X THE LARRY WILDE
　　　　　　BOOK OF LIMERICKS　　$2.25

____ 20111-5 THE OFFICIAL LAWYERS
　　　　　　JOKE BOOK　　$2.25

____ 14751-X THE OFFICIAL DOCTORS
　　　　　　JOKE BOOK　　$2.25

____ 14623-8 *More* THE OFFICIAL SEX
　　　　　　MANIACS JOKE BOOK　　$1.95

____ 14349-2 THE *Last* OFFICIAL
　　　　　　JEWISH JOKE BOOK　　$1.95